Village Stories

edited by Liam Stewart

the village storytelling centre

First published in 2005 by
The Village Storytelling Centre
St. James (Pollok) Parish Church
183 Meiklerig Crescent
Glasgow G53 5NA

10 9 8 7 6 5 4 3 2 1

Copyright © 2005

The publishers acknowledge funding from:

Greater Pollok Social Inclusion Partnership
through the Scottish Executive Integration Fund
and Glasgow City Council Culture and Leisure
Arts for Social Work Service Users

ISBN: 0-9547491-1-1

Printed by Clydeside Press, Glasgow

Contents

Introduction   5

Londi Beketch Luyeye (D.R. Congo)
A Special Recipe   7
Hunting Disaster   12
The Radio and the Clock   17
An Accident   19
Loose Cannon   21
The Walking Pub   22

Louise Goodall (Scotland)
First Days   23
The Blue Vase   28
The Glesga Entrepreneur   30
Feed the Birds   34

Sarita Aranja (Afghanistan)
Kandahar   38
Mash   40
Self Defence   42

Bill Lambie (Scotland)
The Good Old Days?   44
The Tank   48

Florence Odaru (D.R. Congo)
Grasshoppers   52
Upside-Down Day   53

Farnaz Hasibi (Iran)
No Freedom for Women   56
Guilty Mother   59
A Lovely Day for the Wedding   64

Sunil Aranja (Afghanistan)
Good Days   67

Ahlam Souidi (Algeria)
Prisoners in Freedom   70
Eid il-Fitr   76
Faisal   79
Tea or Coffee   81
Mohamed is Rescued   83

Zeynep Gunay (Turkey)
Kayser City   85

Jesrina Nasar (Sri Lanka)
Twenty Four Hours to Leave   88

David Paul (Iran)
His Grandfather's Hands   91
In the Garden   95
The Baby   98

Introduction

Do you remember the house you grew up in? Can you bring it back to life through your senses: the cooking smells from the kitchen (black pudding? ash poshtepah? the celebration cakes?), the sounds from the street (a rattling tramcar, goats on their way to market, the call to prayer), the play of light on jars and pots with their shapes and colours and textures, the heat of the fire on your face, the cold flagstones on your soles, the feel of wool, cotton, silk. What about the neighbours? The ones who warmed your insides with soup and kindness, the ones who stepped out of your storybook of trolls and formed a hazard between you and the safety of home, or the ones who introduced you to stand-up comedy. Or the schools where routine and rote was a rhythm that marched you into responsible adulthood, or the ones where *a* was for anger, *b* was for belt and *c* was for cane. Think again about the strangeness, exhilarating, traumatic, of first days – in the big school, in a new house in Pollok, in a frightening city in a foreign land. Looking back over the decades, which memories hold their hands up demanding to speak? And the present? What is your

Village Stories

life like - here, now, in Glasgow, in Scotland, in this changing world? Unlock your imagination and set it free to travel wherever it chooses, to fall into the company of whoever it meets. Invent, mourn, celebrate, wonder, rage, rejoice!

That's a selection of some of the ideas and starting points for writing that we worked with in our weekly sessions in the Village Creative Writing class. What follows are the memories, reflections, observations, sad stories, funny stories, poems that took legs and walked. Nourished by the experiences of cities and neighbourhoods from around the world (Algiers, Gorbals, Kandahar, Chilaw, Kayser, Kinshasa, Pollok, Teheran), this is an anthology that can be enjoyed for its vitality, its insight and its cultural richness.

Liam Stewart

LONDI BEKETCH LUYEYE

A Special Recipe

Early one morning, the King of the Matata village entered the public meeting place. He was wearing a long, white embroidered boubou, and, attached round his waist was a large bag full of different fruits, cakes, smoked fish and dried meat. This special bag was his overnight supply of food while his servants were away.

Unfortunately, this king was greedy and selfish. 'I have had enough of eating the same dishes,' he shouted. 'My cookery service is the worst in the kingdom. Enough is enough. I want a special recipe. I am the king! Anyone in this village who can do this will bring joy to their king. It is not for me to say

Village Stories

what ingredients you should use or how you should mix them and cook them in order to satisfy me. This would be a recipe for disaster.'

The villagers came forward hesitantly to hear what the king was saying. Then they started gossiping to each other. 'Look at him always eating, eating, eating and eating,' one said. 'He would make eating the national pastime.'

'He's got a big enough stomach,' said another, 'but he hasn't got any good ideas for saving the village or solving all our problems.'

Then one of the king's cooks came forward and said, 'my king, this isn't fair.'

'What do you mean by this?' said the king.

'I mean every day we do our best to satisfy our king. We go far looking for special food. Sometimes we have accidents, sometimes we are bitten by snakes or stung by bees while we are picking fresh fruit. But you don't even care. All you do is tell people what bad cooks we are. You care only about yourself.'

The king couldn't believe what he was hearing. 'Where do you get such boldness to talk to me like this? Who are you? Never mind. I have something more important to sort out at the moment than to teach you a lesson. Guards! Guards! Take him away!'

'No, my king! I am one of your cooks. I just wanted to show you how much we care about you!'

'Guards! I said take him away! Put him in the cave. He will be out of the way until I find a special recipe. And the rest of you, I am warning you: do not behave like him. From now, the competition is open to all people living in this village, without exception. Bring me a special recipe! The one who succeeds will live with me in the palace for ever. Your time starts now. Go!'

Among the villagers, there was a man who was dressed in rags. The villagers called him 'Mobola' which means 'poor'. But his real name was 'Nsoti' which means 'frog', because he liked catching and eating frogs. Apart from his dog, he hadn't a friend in the village. When he heard the proclamation, he said to himself, 'this is a good opportunity for me to show everybody that we are all important in this village.'

In the evening, with his torch, net and plastic bag, Nsoti walked down to the river. Evening is the best time to catch frogs. As usual, his dog helped him, running everywhere along the bank, in the grass, shaking the small trees, jumping into the river to chase the frogs from their hiding places. Once he

Village Stories

had done this, it was easy for Nsoti to catch them in his net.

After a long night, Nsoti returned home with a good catch of frogs. First of all, he cut them in pieces and cleaned them. Then he dug some fresh potatoes from his garden. 'Hm,' he said, 'I have never done it this way before. But the king wants a special recipe, so I will just cook the frogs' legs with potatoes and onions and wrap them all in banana leaves.'

Then he tied a knot in the leaves and put them under the fire and waited about one hour for them to be cooked. After that he went to sleep to be ready for the big moment the next day.

In the morning, the sun was high, the birds were singing and the children were running about in the playground. The public meeting place was tidied and all the villagers were gathered. A minute later the king appeared, looking anxious.

'The time is up,' he said. 'I didn't eat all night. So bring me the dishes made from your special recipes.'

One by one the villagers came forward carrying their recipes and their dishes, and the king tasted each one. At each tasting, he shook his head. None was any good. None was unusual. 'Rubbish!' he said after each one. At the end he shouted, 'they were all rubbish!'

Then suddenly a dog started barking and ran to the front of the crowd. Everyone recognised Nsoti's dog, but Nsoti was nowhere to be seen. It lay down at the king's feet and everyone could see attached to its back was a recipe.

'Whose dog is this?' asked the king.

'Nsoti's,' said the villagers.

'Why is he ashamed to show me his recipe? Why does he send his dog?'

'Because he is poor and is dressed in rags.'

'I want to see him. All have to participate, without exception.'

Then one of the villagers went to find Nsoti and tell him the king wanted to see him urgently. Nsoti couldn't believe it. He went to meet the king right away, carrying the dish with him.

'Why are you hiding yourself?' said the king. 'Open up this recipe and tell me its name.'

Nsoti unfolded the recipe from the dog's back and handed it to the king.

'My king, it is called 'Liboke'. It is a simple dish, made with frogs' legs and potatoes. I have eaten it all my life. I think you will like it.'

'Liboke? Frogs' legs? An unusual dish!'

The king was surprised to see what was in the

Village Stories

recipe. He took the plate from Nsoti and sampled the Liboke. After a moment, he said, 'Hmm.... Liboke? Yes, Nsoti, with this dish of frogs' legs and potatoes, you are the winner.'

Nsoti wondered if he had heard correctly.

'Me? The winner!?

'Yes, said the king 'The outright winner.'

'Now we will change your name to Turkey,' said the villagers, 'because now you are a celebrity!'

'Thankyou, my king. This special recipe has saved my life and raised me up.'

'Now,' said the king, 'from now on, all the cooks apart from Nsoti will be catching frogs and bringing them to him, because now he is Cookery Manager. And his dog is Assistant Manager.'

Hunting Disaster

There are many different cultures in the world, each with its own way of educating the next generation. My parents and grandparents gave me a lot of advice about how to find my way round the obstacles I faced. I have many memories, but the hunting trip, when I was thirteen, stands out as one of the most exciting.

It was five o'clock on a Saturday morning, when my brother came into my bedroom and said, 'Londi, it's time to go. Wake up!' He folded my mosquito net, pulled out my bedsheet and tugged my leg.

'Oh no!' I said. 'It's still night. Give me ten minutes to finish my dream.'

'No, Londi! The others are waiting for us outside!'

I pulled the pillow over my ears and started to snore. 'Krooo! Krooo!'

'Come on,' my brother said. 'This is for your future. I have already passed this test. It is time for you to move and jump like an antelope.'

This got through to me and I hauled myself out of bed. I had a cup of juice and then, after quickly showering and brushing my teeth, I left the house.

'At last!' said my friends.

We took a bus out of town and then we walked miles into the forest to where we could find birds and animals. The forest was full of sounds: birdsong, the noise of insects and the calls of monkeys and other creatures.

In our party, there were seven adults, four teenagers and three dogs. 'Two adults and one dog will

Village Stories

accompany the three boys, and they will go and catch birds,' said the elder. 'Remember, do not use your catapults. We want the birds alive for the cage. So, you must use your intelligence. The other group will be hunting animals.'

A minute later, we walked on to an open grassy area, near the valley where birds were having a sun-bathe. Right away, I saw a big brown, yellow, red and black bird ready to go into the water. I told my friend, 'this is mine.' So, I lay down on the ground and covered myself with leaves to hide myself from the bird. Then I crawled towards it, very slowly, like a snake.

I was only about one metre away from the bird, just ready to jump, when suddenly another hunter raised its head right in front of me. It was a big snake and it was poised to bite me! Summoning all the energy I could, I sprang to my feet and ran. Behind me I saw the grass shaking and I realised the snake was coming after me. I ran and ran, crying for help. When I got close to my friends, they shouted, 'what happened?'

'Nioka! Nioka!'

'But there isn't any snake behind you!' they shouted.

'Well, there was,' I replied and I told them what had happened.

But, after a couple of minutes, I decided to go back into action because I really wanted one of that kind of bird. Suddenly I saw it flying in the other direction and going into hiding in a small tree. I knew it was a bird that cannot fly more than two miles without having a break.

So I talked to my heart, telling it at that moment, the snake couldn't make me afraid, and I walked, ran and jumped over the stream to where I had seen the bird. Then I crawled forward, and saw him eating seeds. Very slowly, removing dead twigs from

Village Stories

my path to reduce the cracking noises, I crept forward. I got closer and closer and then I jumped up and grabbed at the bird and caught him by the legs. Unfortunately, as I did so, a bee's nest fell from the tree and the bees flew out and started to sting me. I ran as fast as I could, holding on to the bird by the legs and grabbing small branches to chase away the bees.

After running a few miles, I joined my colleagues with a swollen face that made them all start laughing at me. While we were sharing our adventures with each other, the other group (the five adults, one boy and two dogs) were involved in some big danger. When they returned, they told us they had been surprised by a big, black cat. Thanks to the dog, they managed to scramble up into a tree. But sadly, after a short combat, the dog was killed while the adults from the safety of the tree tried to shoot the big cat with their catapults. Shortly afterwards, the cat had run away.

As we put all the birds we had caught into the cage for sale, we felt sad about the loss of the dog. It had been a hunting disaster. But although I felt sad about it all, it helped me build confidence, patience, observation, listening and agility.

The Radio and the Clock

My dad liked antique things. Two that he valued in particular were an old radio and an alarm clock. I was about ten years old when he bought them from an antique shop. Both things were very funny in the way they operated.

The radio was huge, about a meter and a half wide and approximately two meters in height. It was dark brown in colour and it occupied the left-hand corner of the living room. It looked like a small cupboard with two doors.

After a long working day, my father usually lay down in the sofa and opened the two doors of the radio. Attached to each door was a large, family photo, one of my Mum on the right-hand door and one of my Dad on the left-hand door. It gave a great dimension to the living-room. Then my Dad would turn on the radio and it would start with a funny rhythmic sound like a duck. The radio itself had six buttons, one for tuning, one for volume, and four for bands, and also a light. The sound was as loud and strong as a live musical band.

One day the radio broke down and my father took it to be repaired. Unfortunately, the electrician said

Village Stories

that the fuses were blown and that kind of fuse was rare in the market and was no longer being made. He promised that he would do what he could to repair it but he did not tell my father that he was moving home soon.

A month later, my father went to find out if he had got the fuses, only to discover that that there was nobody there. He was told that the electrician had moved house. My father was angry about what had happened. 'I wanted to keep that radio at home,' he said, 'because it was a special one and could have been exhibited in a museum.'

The alarm clock was a big one that was attached to the wall above the TV. When the alarm rang, the small door opened and a cartoon of a man popped out laughing, 'Ha! Ha! Ha!' All my sisters and brothers started laughing too because it was great fun for young ones. And do you know what my father did? He cut out a portrait of himself and stuck it on the cartoon character. This meant that when the clock rang, my father's face popped out instead of the cartoon man. It gave visitors a great laugh. I don't know where that clock went, because eventually I left the family home to set out on my own life.

An Accident

*W*here am I? I know I was on the zebra crossing and then something happened to me. A bicycle knocked me down. I was unconscious. Everything is quiet here: there's a smell of medicine, there's pain in my body, my face is covered in bandages and I can't move my leg because my thigh is injured and my knee is swollen. The doctor told me, 'don't worry, there are no bone fractures. You have a wound in your thigh; we have stitched it and in a couple of days, you can go back home, when we have controlled your temperature.'

My mum looks after me, and she can't sleep at night because my pain makes her cry. Sometimes I turn my head and look out the window. Life continues for others, but mine has stopped for a week as I lie in this hospital bed.

*

In my bedroom, I am sad because I did something bad. In the kitchen, I tried to make a cup of tea, but I couldn't do it because my hands were shaking and my legs were frozen. I open my windows for fresh air but it can't cool me down, because my mind is

Village Stories

switched on and I watch the accident I caused and I realise how serious it was. I batter my pillow and scream. It was my fault because the bike was too big for me. My father comes into the bedroom and says, 'did this happen because I didn't buy you a bike on time and teach you how to ride it, and instead you took mine? Well, your new bike is here, outside.'

'No! No, Dad! I have given up riding. After that experience I will never ride a bike again.'

*

The ward door opens and a man in his forties walks in carrying a bunch of pink, red and blue flowers. He comes to my bed and sits down. His face looks worried and kind. He holds my hand and says, 'sorry for what my son did to you. It wasn't his fault, it was mine because I didn't buy him a bike that was the right size for him, so he always stole mine. We are sorry. These flowers are for you.'

'Thankyou,' I say, 'I am feeling better now. Don't be worried. I should also look carefully before I cross.'

Loose Cannon

I travelled long days and nights through hills and valleys accompanied by horses and soldiers singing the victory song of war. I felt sad about what we had done in destroying the only castle that Pollok had, its greatest treasure.

One day, while I was on tour near the ruins of the castle, a group of local people recognised me and said, 'we know you. You are the one who destroyed our Crookston Castle. Now we will destroy you!'

'No! No!' I said, but I couldn't defend myself against those angry people, who started to follow me with stones and tree trunks. I fell down and they stamped on me. I couldn't do anything because I didn't have the power that I had before. The security forces came and rescued me, and I was taken on a journey to where I belong – banished to Edinburgh Castle. Now people take photos of me because I was a particular master of destruction.

Village Stories

The Walking Pub

It is a deep, dark evening.
Buses, taxis, ambulances, fire engines, police cars
    are passing.

He walks here, there,
Bottles and cans in his big coat pocket make noises
    to the rhythm of his stumble.

'Will the day return soon?' he says. But he can't
    find the way.
He staggers over path and road, singing and
    vomiting.
He jumps up and says: 'La vie est belle!'

If life is good, why are you stumbling?

Because I am a walking pub!

LOUISE GOODALL

First Days

I remember feeling very important when I reached the age of eleven. Not only did I have a lovely party, but I learned later that I now counted as 'points'. The points system was used by the Housing Department of the City Council to help prioritise each family's place in the housing list. I was now old enough to add points to our total. It meant our family had high hopes of moving to one of the large housing schemes that had been popping up all over the outskirts of the city for the last few years. We were soon able to arrange an exchange with another family. After two years of living 'out of town,' they were very keen to get back to the city

Village Stories

centre to be near all the shops and amenities once again. My head was so full of the excitement of having a new house I could not understand why they would want to move back into an old house. We had always lived in a tenement building and been happy there, so we had only the vaguest idea of what the new house would be like. But I could tell that Mother and Father had high hopes of this very exciting event.

The first days were great fun for the children. 'Look! Look what I've found!' we called to each other as we ran all over the house. Our voices echoed in the big and almost empty rooms. The shout came back, 'I'm out the back door. There's grass and a shed,' followed by, 'can we play out now? Pleeease!'

'Not now,' said Mother, 'come and see your room.'

We gazed in awe at the large room that was to be ours: two rooms and a great view over the hills. In the old house, my sister and I had shared the 'hole in the wall' bed in the kitchen recess and so the new room was in itself a big adventure to us. It was not until I was older I realised how much work was involved for our parents in this 'flitting' and how busy those days were.

Our furniture seemed sparse in such spacious

rooms. The big windows made everywhere seem light and airy. But, we soon got used to the space and gradually the rooms filled up with our own special treasures. I remember we had a wind-up gramophone with very old vinyl and plastic records, and, when the singing slowed down, you had to wind the handle quickly to speed up the song or it faded away altogether.

On lighter nights we were allowed out to play and all the children in the street shouted out for their favourite games. Cries of, 'let's play ropes'; 'naw kick the can's better'; 'I want tae play hide an' seek' could be heard ringing out over the laughter and fun of just being together. Our first winter was really cold. Snow lay on the ground for days and days. Here in Pollok was our very own winter wonderland. My breath froze as I spoke and my nose tingled with cold. I had seen snow before, but in the city streets it turned to slush in no time at all. Here we had time to play. I remember putting on wellies and two sets of gloves for throwing snowballs, and venturing forth. We built a snowman with coal for eyes, an old carrot for a nose and five stone buttons down his middle. Then we added a scarf to keep him warm. I loved my first ride on a sledge and the freedom to race downhill

Village Stories

was scary and fun at the same time: snow stinging my cheeks and a tumble out at the bottom. Breathless and red-cheeked, all wet and soggy, we eventually went home to a hot drink and a heat in front of the coal fire.

In our new house, my mother's chief delight was having her own back green to hang out her washing. The days spent booking a place at the steamie were in the past. There was a boiler, two big, deep sinks with a grey wringer in the middle to rinse out the washing. The Monday morning smell of the newly-boiled sheets being squished through the big rollers of the wringer was the signal of the start of a new week. When the sheets were brought in from the back green, they smelled of fresh air and wind – nothing quite like it.

Talking about the steamie reminds me of the public hot baths that were attached to that building. Before our new house days, we went on bath nights to the Hot Baths. I really disliked it there, whether it was the thought of having to be clean or the fear of the lady in charge, who loomed over us with keys jangling at her waist. She always had the water far too hot and yelled constantly: 'Hurry up! Hurry up!' or 'Time's up!' and rapped on the doors as she strode up and down the rows of cubicles. The walk home was no better; it always seemed so cold after the heat indoors. The luxury of our new bathroom was just that – our own bath. To take as much hot or cold water as we liked and to make as much noise and take all the time we wanted! Oh yes, the new house was tops in so many ways!

Father, although he worked late some nights and always on Saturday mornings, was fast becoming a keen gardener. He worked hard and soon had fine flower beds at the front of the house. In the back garden, he planted potatoes and vegetables. Nothing tasted so good as the potatoes you were allowed to dig up yourself. It seemed to take longer to cook than any other meal but the new potatoes dripping with butter were fit for a king. Father joined the local gardeners' group and became quite an expert. Roses were his speciality. He loved to pass on tips about the plants to fellow gardeners among the neighbours. We all took part in the local flower shows at the community centre and soon had quite a collection of certificates for baking, painting, flower arranging and flowers and vegetables of all kinds. How proud we were of our exhibits on the day of the show! Win or lose, it was all the same.

Village Stories

Our first summer in Pollok was full of great discoveries: learning to name the trees and the flowers; finding the shady parts of the woods where the bluebells made a lovely carpet beneath our running feet, seeing for the first time the flowering cherry trees edging the sides of the wide roads, with the pink blossoms fluttering down all around like summer snow. We spotted the first snowdrops in mother's wee rockery, followed by daffodils and crocuses. Yes, there were so many firsts for us city children to learn about. A time full of happy memories.

The Blue Vase

As a child, I often visited my granny's house with my mother. Granny sat beside the big, black range in the kitchen, always wearing black, head to toe, and with an apron wrapped around her. She also wore a mutch cap, made of cotton and elasticated all round the edges to keep her hair in place. She had a wonderful head of real, silvery hair, so long she could sit on it – or so I was told. I never saw this miracle of nature for myself. Still I was most impressed by the idea of such long tresses. Despite having her own house to look after and four children, my mother tidied, cleaned and shopped for Granny, and prepared an evening meal for her two younger brothers: they were working but still stayed with Granny. Mother also regularly black-leaded the range and re-set the fire for later in the day. The house was a two apartment flat in a grey tenement with a big room that had a large fireplace. I don't remember ever seeing a fire lit in that room, but I do remember the beautiful, blue vases, a matching pair that stood at either end of the very high mantelpiece. In my eyes, these vases, safely out of the reach of eager, young fingers, looked beautiful. I have never been fond of blue as a colour, but this iridescent blue, shot with purples and greens with exotic birds painted on, had a special appeal for me. Granny's kitchen had a shelf all round with many blue and white plates displayed. None of these attracted me. They seemed cold and uninteresting. But the blue vases were special. When I think about this, I am reminded of a poem I learnt at school, 'The Green Glass Beads.' This ended with a passionate plea: 'Those green glass beads, I love them so. Give them me, Give them me. No!' In spite of the repeated re-

Village Stories

quests, the cool answer by the owner of the beads and simple refusal to part with them struck me as quite daring.

I now associate this pride of ownership with my beautiful blue vase, as, when my Granny died, I became the guardian of one blue vase, and my sister of the other. I feel I could say *No* to any request to take it from me. It is an object of little value to others, yet for me, it represents memories of childhood and evokes many different thoughts of being comforted, cared for and much loved. All of this wrapped up in my beautiful blue vase.

The Glesga Entrepreneur

Wee John wis jist seven years old, quick as a whippet and nearly as thin. His mammy let him use the old pram wheels. Efter a' his wee sister wis walkin noo and didnae need the pram. He rushed in fae school, threw his satchel in the corner and dashed oot again grabbin the pram wheels fae the close heid as he went. It wis Monday washday. If he hurried he'd get tae the steamie in plenty time.

A bit breathless but actin very casual he says, 'Oh hullo, Mrs Murphy. Is that yir washin a' finished? Can ah help ye up the road wi' it?'

'Aw, son that wid be great. That bundle therr. The wan tied up wi' the blue and white tablecover.'

John heaves the bundle on tae the empty pram. He rattles and clanks along beside Mrs Murphy. She stays two doors up fae his granny's hoose and only wan stair up. He might nip in and get a jammy piece at his granny's in the passin. 'How's Mr Murphy daein?' says wee John.

'Well, he's no sae bad,' says Mrs Murphy. 'He's wheezy like and no oot much but his spirits is good considerin whit he went through when he wis away at the fightin'.

Village Stories

'That's fine,' says John. No far to go noo, but his heart sinks. Here's Mrs Murphy's freen stopping for a blether. They staun talkin oan and oan. John's hoppin fae foot tae foot. It's getting a bit caulder noo. 'Could ah go ahead and take yir washin up the stair?' he asks when there's a wee pause in the gossip.

'Aye okay son. Oan ye go. Ah'll no be lang.'

John humphs the washing up the stair. The bundle's the same size as him near enough. He leaves it on the doormat and rings the bell. He disnae wait for he knows the man o' the hoose takes a while to reach the door. Back doon the stairs two at a time and oot oan tae the street he goes. Whit noo? Nae sign o' Mrs Murphy. He hurls the empty pram in front o' him, wonderin if his granny wid be in yet. As the pram bumps along on the cobbles, there's a shout fae the butcher's shop. 'Hing oan, son, ah'll be oot in a minute.'

Mrs Murphy had nipped in tae get a bit square slice for her man's tea. So that's where she goat tae, thought John. 'Here's a thruppenny bit for yir trouble, John. You're a good lad. Ah wis telling Boab the Butcher yir a real wee entre… …well. Whit's the word? Yir a great wee help oanyway.' Boab says an entre… whatever it is, is whit his nephew hud in a posh restaurant when he wis in America. I think he's haverin masel.'

John races back tae the steamie – still in time. Here's Mrs McConaghy comin oot noo. 'Can ah gie ye a haun, Mrs? Ah've goat ma bogie wi' me.'

'Thanks. Ah don't feel like cairryin that wet washin up the road masel.'

'You're up the hill a bit noo and it's the tap flat isn't it?' says John

'Aye, we're three up noo, that's right. We jist moved last week,' says the wifie.

'Is your Denis comin oot tae play fitba' later oan?' asks John.

'Maybe. Ah'll see efter he's hud his tea if it's no too dark.'

John struggles up three flights of stairs and meets Mrs McConaghy on the first landing on his way back doon. 'Here's a silver sixpence. That was a big load ye took up the day.'

'Thanks. Ah'll come back up fur Denis later,' he shouts, disappearin back oan tae the street. He dashes back to the steamie door, and there's his next customer, Mrs Broon, likely the last the night. The steamie will be closing noo.

Village Stories

She's bent near double wi' age. 'Gie's yir bundle o' washin, it's only a wee drap. It'll go in the pram nae bother.' John knows it's no far up the road and it's a low door hoose.

'Here ye are, sonny.' Mrs Broon gies him a shiny penny.

John thinks aboot getting a penny dainty at the shop and smiles at Mrs B. 'See ye next week,' says he.

He jingles the coins in his pocket and whistles, a bit oot o' tune. 'I wunner whit an entre- whatever it is can be?' he thinks, as he makes his way back to his ain hoose.

Feed the Birds

A young woman sat quietly on a bench in the City Centre square. She enjoyed this peaceful oasis despite the hum and bustle of the traffic on all sides. The grass, flowers and trees seemed to push the busy-ness of the day away as the early evening sun spread across the patterned stone at her feet.

Helena drew breadcrumbs from a brown paper bag and threw them down. In seconds the pigeons were strutting, pecking, jostling for their share. Then, having cleared the space before her, they fluttered off to find their next benefactor. She smiled thoughtfully as she watched, remembering a time some two years before. Her mum sobbing as Helena held her in her arms. 'I hate all birds. They nearly killed my boy. They'll get no more crumbs from me. I'd like to poison them all.'

'Mum, don't upset yourself so,' said Helena. 'How was Jim when you left the hospital?'

'Oh, he was a little easier, but not saying much and only able to move his arms. The doctors say they hope he will improve given time. Those dreadful birds!' she added on another bitter sob.

Her brother Jim had come to a bend in the road when a flock of birds, gathering to migrate for the winter, had streamed up out of the hedgerows. Jim had been unable to see clearly and he jerked the wheel and crashed into an oncoming vehicle. The other driver, who wasn't so badly hurt, said the crash couldn't have been avoided. Months passed with little improvement in Jim, but, even hurt as he was, he saw the change in Mum. She became obsessed with blaming all the problems on the birds. After long days spent at the hospital, she often cried out

Village Stories

her frustration at the birds in our back garden. She shooed them off with some violence; it seemed to relieve the tension all the family felt.

The doctors and physios were worried. Jim seemed listless, uninterested in helping himself to recovery. Until one spring morning he indicated he wanted paper and a pencil. Then he began to sketch a little robin who sat posing cheekily on the hospital window ledge. The bird seemed aware of the attention he was receiving.

He showed the sketch to Mum, hoping she would let go of her feelings of bitterness. 'Why draw a bird?' she asked, 'You used to be so good at doing cartoon characters.'

But Jim's interest was sparked. He worked at his exercises with the physios, and they were delighted with his progress. He continued to sketch. The birds obligingly continued to appear on the window ledge: sparrows, wagtails, blue tits and, occasionally Mr Robin himself. At Jim's bedside, the pile of sketches grew. One day, a passing visitor took an interest.

'These are really good,' he said. 'I'm producing a children's book. It's to be published soon. These drawings could be the finishing touches I need to enhance the story! Would you be interested in helping?'

That was the turning point for Jim. Soon he was able to get back home and be full of purpose again. He sat in the garden producing detailed, colourful sketches of the birds that visited. But, as soon as he was indoors, Mum dashed outside and shooed those birds away; they were still not welcome in her world.

It was late summer now and Helena felt life was getting back to a more normal routine. As she looked up, she saw her mum and Jim walking towards her, arm in arm. The shadows lengthened in the square and she watched as Mum laughed happily at some remark of Jim's. Helena's smile broadened as she noticed Mum held in her hands a small brown bag full of breadcrumbs and hope for the future.

The bitterness was gone, her son restored to her. The birds forgiven at last.

Village Stories

SARITA ARANJA

Kandahar

When I was young in Kandahar, my father and his two partners ran a clothes business, taking goods to sell round different shops. Kandahar was like a big village, and it would have been a fine, sunny place to live if it hadn't been for the war. When the Russians came to Afghanistan, one of the things they used to do was to capture boys as young as sixteen and make them into soldiers. I remember we kept one of my brothers safe at home when he was sixteen, and another brother went to Kabul for his studies. If he had stayed in Kandahar and they saw him walking on the road, they could just have picked him up. They asked nobody's permission. They would keep the boys in the army for three years and after that they would give them a certificate.

Then the Taliban came to power. Now we had to wear clothing that completely covered us from head to toe. We had a net to breathe through but it was very hot and uncomfortable. When we went shopping, we could take the thing off our face so that we could see what we were buying, but that was all. It was better with the Russians because, despite the military service, they helped people. They brought things we didn't have, like tinned foods, which they would give to boys to give to their families.

The Indian Embassy was near where we lived. People used to come and work there for a couple of years and we got to know them. I remember one night in our house, one of our neighbours making a tape recording of the gunfire so that he could take it back to India to show people what life was like in Kandahar.

Village Stories

Mash

There was once a boy called Mash who lived with his mother and father and his three brothers and two sisters. He was a very nice and lovely boy and he loved everybody in his family. But most of all, he loved his youngest sister. When she cried, Mash cried because he loved her so much. He used to say, 'my sister is the best sister in the world.'

One day, in the holidays, his sister went to her aunt's house, while Mash stayed at home. He was a good boy who never refused to do any of his chores in the house. Every day he went to buy the bread, and he would go by bike. One day he went as usual on his bike and, while he was riding along, something happened and he fell off. When he got to his feet, he wasn't hurt, but, for some reason, he had forgotten everything. The only thing that he could remember was his way home. When he arrived back at his house, he had no bread with him. His clothes were covered with mud but, apart from that he seemed alright. When his parents asked him what had happened, he didn't say anything; he just asked where his sister was. His parents told him that she was at her aunt's house, but he just asked the same question over and over and his parents kept giving the same answer.

Eventually, Mash's parents took him to the doctor. The doctor checked him over and did all the tests to try to find out what was wrong. But nothing changed: he asked only where his sister was. The doctor suggested that the parents should bring his sister to him.

So Mash's father went to the aunt's house to bring his daughter home. When he arrived there, the first thing he noticed was that his daughter was crying. When he asked her aunt why she was crying, she replied that she had no idea. The girl had been crying since the day before and saying that she wanted to go back home to her brother. Her brother loved her so much that they were connected, heart to heart.

Village Stories

Self Defence

One summer, when I was about ten, the weather was warm and bright and, though the war was still on, things seemed quite peaceful. At that time, my father would sometimes send dried fruit to Kabul. Compared to Kandahar, there wasn't much of this in Kabul, so people did this kind of business.

At that time, when people travelled from Kandahar to Kabul, it took two days. They would start at six o'clock one day and usually arrive about the same time two days later. That summer, my father had sent my brother to Kabul to sell the fruit. He had arrived in Kabul within the two days, and things had gone fine and he had started his journey back home to Kandahar. But ten days later he still hadn't returned home. We were all very worried because we didn't know where he was. We knew he had got on the bus, but we didn't know what had happened after that.

After ten days, I was sitting with my family and we were all talking about my brother, when suddenly one of our neighbours came running up to us, hitting herself and crying: 'Something has happened to our children!' Her son was on the same bus. My father asked her what had happened and she told us the boys were travelling from Kabul and on the road, some people had thrown a bomb on to the bus and now our boys were in hospital.

We hurried to the hospital, all of us very upset. My brother was injured in his back, his legs and his hand, but he was not so horribly wounded as some of the others. He told us that the journey had started happily, but after two days, the bus broke down and there was no garage anywhere near to help them. So they spent three or four nights on the road. Then some people came by in a van and helped them to get the bus started and they continued their journey and got quite near Kandahar. By this time, all their food was finished and some of the passengers felt very hungry. So when they saw a tent, a little bit away from the road, some of the younger ones got off the bus and started walking towards it. Suddenly there was a huge noise and they all fell flat on the ground. When they woke, they were in hospital: some had lost their memories, some had lost limbs.

My father got the story about what had happened from a policeman. Apparently, the man responsible for the attack had seen the young men coming towards the tent and thought they were making an attack. So, in self defence, he had thrown the bomb that injured all these young men.

Village Stories

BILL LAMBIE

The Good Old Days?

I was born in Springburn and lived there till I was six, when we moved to the Gorbals. My mother had died when I was one year old and, before the Gorbals move, my father had re-married. We lived in Crown Street and then Cumberland Street, and then, just before I got married we moved to Pollok. It was a short stay: once I was married I was back to Gorbals again.

Gorbals was a good place to live. Up our stair, there were all religions and none: my father claimed to be a Wesleyan atheist because he liked the hymns. There was a Jewish couple, three Irish Catholic families (one first generation, two second) and on the top floor there was a house that belonged to the Salvation Army. It was a captain's house for officers that came to the area for a short period.

We stayed in three different houses up that stair. It was the stair where my sisters, Cathy and Louise were born. You didn't live in your neighbours pockets, but they were there if you needed them. Next door to us, there were the Connachans. I remember Mrs Connachan lost a wee boy from one of the childhood illnesses, whether it was diphtheria or one of the others, I don't remember. But, because of her loss, the parish priest was visiting frequently, and, often as not when I came home from school, he would be in our house talking to my mother. She would meet him and say, 'Mrs Connachan's not in just now. She'll be back shortly, come on in.' There was no bigotry – we were all neighbours.

There were certainly characters too: Abey that wasnae the full shilling - we used to run after him in the street and torment him. It wasn't nice, but kids do that kind of thing; Mrs O'Neill, an enormous, fat woman (I thought she was old, but she was probably in her late forties at the time) who always sat in her window on the ground floor, with the window

Village Stories

open, arms folded on the sill, day after day. She was a great character. All the kids used to go and speak to her and she would say, 'who wants a piece and jam?' There might be five or six boys or girls and they would all get a piece. She fed the neighbourhood kids; old Mrs Rooney who looked like the proverbial witch with her long fingers and big nails that weren't very clean. We were a wee bit frightened of her. She would send you to the shop round the corner for a quarter ounce of snuff. We went for her snuff right enough, but she never gave you anything.

The notion of 'the good old days' in Gorbals can certainly be overstated: the claim that you could leave your door open, for instance. If you left your door open in Gorbals, you were nuts. There were burglars about then, just as there are now. There were a lot of other things about as well, things that we don't have now, for example, rife TB; everybody knew somebody who had died of TB or was dying of it. There was also diphtheria, smallpox, scarlet fever – diseases you don't hear about now. But when you're young everything's fine, the summer holidays are long and the sun always shines. (It's true that the older you get the quicker time passes). On the other hand, if there was bigotry about, I never encountered it.

The streets were comparatively traffic-free and, I don't know if it's a myth, children seemed safer then. Nobody had cars. Every day, I walked from Crown Street to Strathbungo School, unless it was pouring with rain and then I got a tramcar.

My father was a maintenance engineer, a good one. He worked in Gray Dunn's Biscuit Factory for several years and then, until he retired, he was with Associated Metal as the engineer in charge with about seven or eight blokes working under him. The company expanded and he expanded with it. With his ILP background, he was always at Mayday gatherings, for a long time as a trade union representative, and there was a period when he was representing his union and I was representing mine.

My brief time in Pollok started in 1950 and lasted till I got married in 1952 (in those days you stayed with the family till you got married). My abiding memory of our first days in Pollok was that it was freezing cold. There was a heating system involving panels running up the side of the fireplace but it wasn't very effective. I used to wake up in the morning with ice on the bedroom windows. My mother had a great talent for self-delusion. 'Oh it's lovely and warm!' she would say. She never felt the cold. For

Village Stories

years, she went about in the middle of winter in sleeveless blouses.

I didn't know anybody in Pollok. My friends were in Gorbals, and, by the time we moved to Pollok, I had met Anne, my wife. And, when you're winching ('courting' to be polite), your girlfriend practically is your social life. We got a lovely wee house in Gorbals, a single apartment with inside toilet in Nicolson Street, up the stair from Anne's mother. In the first two summers of our married life, we went to Butlin's Holiday Camp. Great fun!

The Tank

As I write, I am in my car, parked on the sea front in Ayr. It is a beautiful day, the sky blue, the air crisp and fresh, if a little chilly. The sea is as blue as it gets off the west coast of Scotland. Arran has a white cap of clouds softening its rugged skyline. Looking to the left towards the heads of Ayr, there are many shades of brown, green and beige. Today is the twenty fifth of January, but I can see some bright yellow blossoms on the gorse bushes. All this show of colour reminds me of another time, another place.

It was about forty years ago; I think the month was November. I was employed as a telecoms engineer. My lot that week was to be engaged on what the company called sub-service, in other words, small jobbing. That morning my heart had sunk when I was given an envelope marked 'XYZ Chemicals'. I usually enjoyed my work, but XYZ was not a nice place to work: there were all the unpleasant smells, a lot of dirt and, worst of all, no canteen.

However, when I got to the job, I found that the work was to be done in what was quite a cosy wee office. So, it was fine enough. My job finished, I visited the company's engineer to get a signature for the work done. He signed my sheet and then said, 'By the way Bill, there's something else. Could you look at it?'

In accordance with my company policy, I agreed. So he took me to the back door of the office and pointed towards a tiny building about three hundred yards away. 'We would like to have a phone in that pump-house,' said he.

For the second time that day, my heart sank. I could barely make out the building indicated. It lay

Village Stories

on the far side of a scene of utter desolation. Some years previously, the older parts of the factory had been removed from this area, and the site had never been properly cleared.

It was a dreadful day. It was cold, it was misty, it was a real, depressing, dirty, dreich, Glesga day. Between me and the pump-house lay an industrial wilderness of half-demolished, twisted and rusty steelworks, broken down cranes, mud and muck. Nevertheless I had to make my way through all this dereliction to find a practical cable route. As I progressed towards my objective, I grew colder and more depressed, my natural optimism completely vanquished, and a voice within me muttering, 'why me?'

I had got about halfway to the pump-house, when I came across a rectangular tank. Like everything else it was in a corroded condition. It was about ten feet long, six feet wide and maybe four and a half feet high. There was no top on it, so, as I passed, I glanced inside. What I saw stopped me in my tracks.

There before me lay an explosion of colour. This container had been used for a long time as a dump for many varied chemicals. The result was an absolutely amazing effect. Every colour one could imagine was there: reds, pinks, blues, brilliant yellow, russet brown, purples, it was as though, Picasso, Chagall and Dali had had an artists' debate at the bottom of this old rusty tank. I don't know who won the fight, but great art does affect me even if it occurs by accident. I was certainly affected, in fact it cheered me and I began to feel a great deal better.

All this had taken place on the banks of the River Clyde and, as I looked around, the thought occurred to me that before industry had besmirched it, this area would really have been quite beautiful. I could imagine willows, birches, alders, bull rushes at the river's edge, birds singing. I had the idle fancy that maybe all the colour leeched from the area had found itself condensed into the bottom of that old tank.

Village Stories

FLORENCE ODARU

Grasshoppers

When I was young, we had a tortoise, a big one of over ten years, which was being kept to be eaten when the time was ripe. To cook a tortoise, you boil water and put the tortoise in. Then the shell will separate from the meat. You can't kill the tortoise before you boil it, because, of course, when you touch it, it draws its head in and you can't get at it. It was common enough to eat tortoises, but I didn't want to eat this one. It had been with me for a long time and I wanted to keep it as a pet. My mother said no, it was going to be cooked. So I said OK, if that's what she was going to do I wasn't going to eat it. It would be like eating a human being - your brother or your sister. I told her I would just eat grasshoppers.

The grasshoppers come at a particular time – something like once in a year. You see a big cloud and then they land on the grass. And the people who live round the area, everyone, including children, come out and pick them. You find them particularly in sorghum: they hide in there and if you open the leaves you can find them. You remove the wings and legs (because they don't taste good), and you fry them a little and then add some oil and some onions and turmeric. In a little while, they turn yellow then orange, and they become crunchy and that's when they are ready to eat.

I've never eaten tortoise.

Upside Down Day

One day Little Clown came into the dining room where Daddy Clown was having breakfast. The cereal that Father Clown was pouring into the

Village Stories

bowl was falling on the floor: the bowl was upside down.

'Dad, look all your cereal's falling on the floor,' said Little Clown.

'Well, today is upside down day.'

Little Clown turned his cup upside down and started to pour milk. All the milk poured on to the floor.

When little Clown went to the playground, all his toys were upside down. While he was playing with them, his friend came to play with him. He was walking upside down.

'Hullo, Little Clown,' Little Clown's friend greeted him.

'Hullo, Friend Clown,' Little Clown answered. 'Why are you walking upside down?'

'It makes things easier,' Friend Clown answered.

Then, instead of playing football, Little Clown and Friend Clown, started hand-throwing the ball. Little Clown saw Mother Clown and Father Clown standing watching them playing.

'It's not really an upside down day, is it Dad?' said Little Clown.

'For us clowns, every day is an upside down day,' Father Clown answered.

They all laughed.

Village Stories

FARNAZ HASIBI

No Freedom for Women

On the old days in Tehran, family and friends were very important for us. We liked to meet each other and celebrate, and the pleasure of these friendships and relationships was one of the central things in our lives. I miss times like that. Another very positive thing was education: in my city it was very important for children. After school, they had to do some homework, not a great deal, but enough, and parents were expected to teach them while they were doing their homework. That's why the parents too had to be educated. The children got used to this routine and they studied more. There was enough time to play and we also had holidays and celebration days. Here I see my children after school, and they have very little homework. My older daughter doesn't have any books at home. She goes to secondary school and she doesn't have any books to read at home. I say to her, 'why are you just sitting on the sofa watching TV?' and she says, 'I haven't any books to read, or any homework to do, because I did all my work at school.' But I think that isn't enough, and that they are wasting time. If they had books to read, it would improve their education.

I was eleven when I went to secondary school. When I was about to start High School, it was the time of the Revolution in Iran. Khomeini came to power and education was suspended. After a time, the schools re-opened, but everything was changed, for example, uniform: now we had to wear a scarf and a long dress in dark colours. You couldn't go straight to university from school: now you had to pass difficult exams. I finished High School when I was eighteen, having missed one year, and I continued to study for the entrance exam. After I took the exam, I was worried about the result, because it was very difficult. It was a big surprise for me when I passed and was accepted for the university to do a law course. The time at university was a good time

Village Stories

for me. I was living in Esfahan, a beautiful, historic city, the second biggest in Iran. I have memories of pleasant times because I had a group of friends the same age as me and we had a lot of fun going around together.

But after the Revolution, many people moved out of the country. Anyone who had worked for the previous regime was in danger of being killed if they didn't get out quickly. It was especially unfair for women.

The law completely changed. There was a new law book. On my course, there were about thirteen women and eighteen men and we argued with the teachers all the time. The law was unfair and we told them so.

Although the course was very difficult to get through, I did pass after four years, because I had to get my certificate. But, after university, I didn't work for a solicitor, because I didn't like the law. I disagreed with the law book. Instead, I worked with children in a secondary school, and I enjoyed it.

The government was very repressive, especially with women. We weren't allowed to get a job as a judge or to work in a court. If, like me, you had done your law course, it was a terrible situation. I'll never forget that time. I had studied hard and gained my qualification but I wasn't allowed to do the jobs that were open to men. The government also banned women from other things they had previously enjoyed doing, taking part in sport, for instance.

So finally, I had problems with the government. I couldn't agree with them. Why should women have these restrictions on them? I asked. Why must women be bound by these laws? It's just not fair I would say. I found myself always in conflict. And finally, I couldn't stand the government. I needed freedom for my opinions. I needed freedom for my children to choose everything they wanted. I have two daughters and I need them to have freedom. I can only hope that things will get better for women in Iran.

Guilty Mother

Twelve years ago when my daughter Noushin was one year old, we decided to hold a big party for her birthday. We were feeling very happy at the prospect of the party. We made a list of all the guests to invite, and another list of all the things we would need. At that time, my husband, Asghar,

Village Stories

worked for a big petrol company, and it so happened that ten days before the party he had to go to the countryside to carry out some emergency work. So, my sister and I went ahead with all the arrangements for the special day. About three days before the party, the phone rang. It was Asghar phoning from the office where he worked. He told me he would have to stay on for another week.

'Are you kidding?' I said

'No, I'm serious,' he said.

I couldn't speak! 'Farnaz!' he said. 'Farnaz, are you still there?' But I didn't answer him. I just put the phone down. Several times he phoned, but I didn't pick up the receiver. There were only two days till the party and we had invited all our friends and family. I had made all the invitation cards! I was so angry with him! How was it going to be possible to cancel the party? My sister offered to go to the houses of people who didn't have phones and I started to phone the others. I spent the whole day phoning. My mother helped by putting away as much as possible of the foodstuffs we had prepared, all the fruit and sweets and everything else. About half of it had to be stored in neighbours' fridges. The next day we took down all the decorations that we had designed ourselves. I will never forget that time, because I was so angry I got ill.

When Asghar returned home, I ignored him. He tried to explain what had happened, but I didn't listen. I was in a huff. The next day he bought new invitation cards and made a new date for the party. He started to prepare everything himself. He ordered a big cake in the shape of a doll and lots of traditional sweets. The day before the party, my family came to help me to get the decorations ready and to tidy up the house and garden.

Everything was ready. I had even bought dresses for Noushin and myself. The one very important thing that I knew nothing about was the food. I asked Asghar, but he just said, 'don't worry.'

On the day of the party I woke up at eight o'clock to the sound of someone knocking on the door. I was worried. Who could it be? Asghar opened the door and said, 'Hi. Welcome! Come in. Let me show you the kitchen.'

I was speechless! My husband had hired a chef and two waiters. He had brought everything he needed to cook for sixty people! It was at that moment, when I was feeling so surprised, that Noushin started to cry. I thought she must need her nappy changed, but, when I picked her up, I realised she

Village Stories

had a temperature. After I gave her some medicine, she improved. Then I left her with my mother so that my sister and I could go to the hairdresser.

When we got back home, there was only one hour to go before the party. I took Noushin to the bedroom to change her nappy and to put on her new dress. She was crying again. I became angry, because I could see she wasn't well. I shouted to Asghar.

'What's wrong with you?' he said.

'It's your fault!' I said. 'If you had been here for the party we had to cancel, everything would have been alright. She was fine then. Look at her now! She isn't well and we have a big party just about to start. What are we going to do?'

As we were arguing, I was changing Noushin's nappy, not paying too much attention. Then, while I was carrying her, our guests started to arrive. The party got underway and everyone was happy and enjoying the dancing. But Noushin was still crying. I didn't know what was wrong with her. I just thought she wasn't well.

At about twelve o'clock after we had finished dinner and eaten the cakes and all the guests had left, Noushin and I were very tired. It had been a big party and everyone had enjoyed it except us.

I took her to the bedroom and changed her nappy. What a shock I got! Round her tummy and her legs her skin was so red! 'Oh my God!' I gasped. 'What's wrong?' Then I realised what had happened. When I had been arguing with Asghar, I had picked up the wrong nappy, one from a packet I had bought by mistake and had been meaning to take back. They were for a new-born baby – far too small for Noushin. That was what had been wrong with her all through her birthday! Once I put some cream on her, she very quickly became relaxed and she slept all through the night till next morning.

Whenever I remember that day, I feel so guilty.

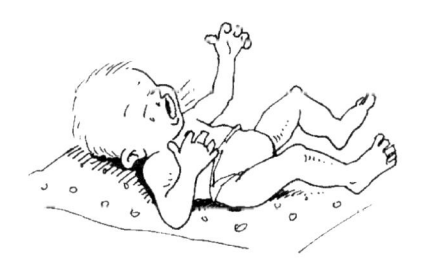

Village Stories

A Lovely Day for the Wedding

In Iranian tradition, a week before a wedding, invitation cards are given out to family and friends. Then the man and woman go shopping for each other: they buy clothes, shoes, jewellery, underwear, make-up, perfume, etc. However, the first day they must buy a big Koran and a special mirror and two lamps or candles that they put beside the mirror. Iranian people believe that, if the mirror breaks, that means the couple will be divorced. That's why they always keep the mirror in a safe place.

After that, the bride and groom go and buy the wedding rings and the wedding dress and suit. The groom's parents book a restaurant for the dinner and arrange for people to serve the guests and look after their needs during the wedding. The day before, fruits and traditional sweeties are prepared. They also go and choose a cake with four or five tiers and prepare the flowers and lights for the wedding decorations.

My story begins on the day before my wedding. It was the first day of autumn. Everything was ready for the next day. The tables and chairs were all arranged round the yard. In the middle beside the pool, there was the big table with all the fruit and sweets with a cover over them.

We were just finishing our dinner and I was saying, 'what perfect weather it is…' But I didn't finish. Suddenly there was a big thunder flash and it started to rain. Within seconds, it was very heavy. We were all shocked, because, in Iran it never rains on the first day of autumn! The only thing we could do was get the fruit and sweets inside.

'It's alright,' my mum said. 'Rain in Iran only lasts for an hour.'

She was right. Sort of! The rain did stop, but then it started to hail! We couldn't believe our bad luck. All we could do was to watch the pool. After a few minutes, my mum said, 'don't worry. It will stop in an hour.'

So it did. It stopped and then it started to snow! My mum didn't say anything, in case what she said would happen. After a few hours, the guests phoned us to ask if the party was still on.

'Yes, of course it is,' we said. 'Don't worry about us. We've got tomorrow as well.'

The truth was that we were worried. I was scared. We slept but it wasn't a peaceful sleep. I got up twice and looked out of the window. It was still snowing.

Village Stories

Finally, I got up at six and got ready. I looked out. It had stopped snowing! I called out the good news, then everybody got up, shouting and laughing. Suddenly, my mother screamed, 'Ah my God!' We ran to her and saw the yard. There was twenty centimetres of snow over everything! 'Can you believe that?' everybody was saying.

'What are we waiting for?' my mum said. 'Come on!' So we all dashed out and started cleaning. We got a couple of big heaters and set them up in the yard to melt the snow. It was my wedding after all! Finally, it was time for me to go to the hairdresser. While I was there, I couldn't speak. I was so worried I was shaking. When I was finished there, I got some photos. Then my husband came to collect me.

When we arrived at our wedding, I was absolutely stunned. Everything was the way I planned. And there were three hundred guests smiling at us. It hadn't been much fun before the wedding, but after that we had the best weather and the best party ever.

SUNIL ARANJA

Good Days

I was born in Kandahar in Southern Afghanistan and I lived there till I was about six years old. Then I moved with my parents to Kabul, the capital city. My father was a priest and, when I was a boy, I used to help him in the temple. As well as keeping the temple clean, I would help to light the little lamps, which we call *arti*. We had to put cotton and oil into the brass container and then light it. During morning and evening prayers, people warm their hands at the flame and then touch their face. This is for a blessing. I didn't go to school. I read at home and a tutor came to teach me every day.

Village Stories

Before the Taliban came to power in Afghanistan, Kabul was a good city to live in. Hindus and Muslims lived together without any trouble. I remember so many enjoyable things from that time in my life. Our neighbours were nice, friendly people and I remember my good friend Sameer. I would often go to his house to play and sometimes I would stay over. His parents were very fine people, always welcoming whenever I came to their house.

There were other memorable things, like the celebrations we had in the temple: good food, family and friends and evenings of singing songs, celebrations for birthdays and many other occasions. Religious festivals were very important to us, for example, Rakhi, Diwali, Guru Nanak.

Rakhi day is the day of brother and sister. The sister knots the thread to her brother's right hand and prays to God for his long life, and the brother asks God to protect and love his sister all her life.

Diwali festival is a very big day for our religion. On that day, we celebrate Sri Ram's birthday. We decorate the house and shops with lights and wear new clothes to pray to Goddess Laxmi. We give out sweets and dried fruits to everybody and we pray for all our family and friends. Afterwards we have a celebration with fireworks and stay up far into the night.

The saddest thing about what happened in Afghanistan was the way people were forced to change their way of life; for instance, women were forced to cover themselves up and wear scarves. This started in 1991 when the Taliban came to power. After that we had a lot of trouble: women could not go outside alone. They were afraid. We tried for two years to leave the country before we finally succeeded. I have other family members who are still there and I miss them very much. Earlier this year, my father passed away, and it grieved me that I could not be there at that time. My mother and brother are still there and I would like to see them.

For now, I hope to gain citizenship in this country. I have already attended the local College and I intend to continue and gain qualifications in Electronics.

Village Stories

AHLAM SOUIDI

Prisoners in Freedom

We ran away from trouble, we ran away from unfairness, from injustice, from killing, from inhumanity, from children burnt in ovens, from the knifing of pregnant women. We ran away from saying yes is no and no is yes, from right is wrong and wrong is right. We ran away from unfairness to fairness, to Britain, to security, to warmth, to justice, because we were hopeful and wished for a better life.

From Heathrow, we went to a friend's house, then

to a hotel in Croydon, and fifteen days later to our destination: Glasgow.

In the bus, there were people from everywhere in the world: Turkey, Algeria, Somalia, Jamaica, Kosovo, all of us wondering what Glasgow would be like and all full of hope. It was Friday morning (after a ten hour bus journey) when we reached Glasgow. We stopped on the outskirts beside a sofa factory, and they asked us to get off and go into the canteen for a cup of tea.

It was only six o'clock and we couldn't see much, but when the sun rose, we got our first view of Glasgow. It was cold and grey. Our hearts sank. All we could see were factories and hills. I started to feel scared. I didn't like Glasgow at all in the beginning.

Our worries continued. We were expecting to be sent to a house but they told us it would be a hotel again. My family and I were the last ones to be assigned to a hotel after waiting six hours. We were so tired from all the travelling and worry and disappointment. They drove us to a hotel somewhere in Glasgow and all the way my tears wouldn't stop. I found Glasgow very different from London. It looked like a dead town, cold and wet and windy, not like the sunny weather we left behind.

Village Stories

The man who was with us didn't concern himself with my tears. He didn't ask anything, just helped us into our room with our bags. I wanted to ask him so many questions about life in Glasgow, but I couldn't because I didn't know any English. All he gave us was a little map of the area, nothing else, no information about doctors or numbers of buses or how to get anywhere or what to do. They just put us in the hotel and left us.

I couldn't stop my tears. All I experienced was disappointment. It was so difficult because we had no knowledge of life in Glasgow. All night I felt cold and fevered. Even when my husband put a lot of blankets on me, it wasn't enough.

Next day I walked sadly along Great Western Road with my husband and my son, Mohammed, exploring the area, and looking for halal food because we were hungry. Suddenly we saw a shop with a sign that said *Baraka*. This means *God bless you* in Arabic. I went in and heard two of the staff talking in what sounded like Algerian! I couldn't believe it. 'Are you Algerian?' I asked in Arabic. 'Oh yes,' the man said, 'are you?'

'Yes,' I replied. I was so pleased and excited. The boss's name was Karim. From my accent, he knew I was from La Casbah, the old city of Algiers, the same area as he came from! His parents had come from the same neighbourhood as my parents! It was as if I had been lost and had now found myself.

He said I looked sad, and asked about our circumstances. We told him our story from beginning to end. He helped us to understand some of the things we were confused by and he encouraged us to face our difficulties. He told us about his own experience since he came to Glasgow a long time ago, and how his life now was very successful. This made me feel stronger.

Two weeks later I went with my husband and my son to the Refugee Council to complain about our circumstances. We wanted a permanent house. We were bored at the hotel: we couldn't cook our own food (there was no kitchen), so we had to buy ready-made food and that was so expensive. The NASS (National Asylum Support Service) official had told us we would only be two or three days at the hotel.

When the day came to move into our own house and be independent, I was so happy. I didn't know the shock that was waiting for us. Two staff from GASS (Glasgow Asylum Support Service) came for us in a van, and we loaded our baggage. The driver was a man who didn't speak to us or smile, and that

Village Stories

gave me a bad feeling. The lady smiled at us all the time, but I felt her smile hid something bad. I was so worried. I looked at my husband. He looked scared. The journey took half an hour and, in that time, we left all the nice houses behind and we entered a poor area that looked empty and cold. Most of the houses were boarded up for demolition. I was already crying. When we stopped, I couldn't get out of the van. The street was like the end of the world. There was nobody about. Everything was silent and dark.

Inside the block, there were two women sitting on the stairs. It didn't seem right, not the kind of behaviour you would expect in a developed country. The lady official opened the door of the flat, on the ground floor, and we went in. It was very small and the walls were in a bad state, damp and cracked. There was no heater. I was still crying, and I told them I couldn't stay there. In such poor accommodation, we would have no quality of life. The lady official just said, 'you'll get used to it,' and left us. They didn't explain to us how we could find a doctor or go shopping or how to get about the city. They didn't seem to care. It was: you don't have a choice. We choose for you until you get your status, then you are free.

For a while, I couldn't open our baggage or do any housework. All we had were food vouchers, but when we went out, we couldn't find any shops that accepted them. The area was very quiet, as if nobody lived in it. After walking for a while, we met some people and they showed us where the shops were and I walked to Sainsbury's and did some shopping. When I got back to the house, I cooked something for dinner, but I couldn't eat anything. I wasn't well. I was angry.

We went to bed about eight o'clock, worried about the future. About nine o'clock we heard some very loud music from our neighbours. They were laughing and shouting and outside people were sitting on the stairs of the entrance and the smell of alcohol was everywhere. They knocked on our door and ran away. These were adults. They put condoms on the handle of the door and through the letter box.

They started to make a lot of trouble for us and we didn't know what to do. I called the police many times, but their behaviour didn't change. I complained to the Council. GASS agreed to give us alternative accommodation in the same area, but it is as well to stay because all the alternatives are worse. We get only one reply: 'No choice until you get your status and then you will be free.' I'm waiting for

Village Stories

freedom. At the moment it is as if we are prisoners in freedom.

Since that time, I have had some good experiences in Glasgow. I have been doing voluntary work and have formed good relationships with nice people. They have allowed me to use my skills and to show that I love to do things for others and to be outgoing. I am very grateful to all the people who have helped me to integrate in Scottish life, particularly to the YMCA staff at Craigbank. (Lesley-Ann, Susan, Selina and Victoria). They have done so much for me and other people who have had to run away from their countries. The YMCA has been like a second family: they have helped me re-find myself.

Eid il-Fitr

I remember very well the preparations for the day of Eid El Fitr. In the last two weeks of Ramadan, my mother would take us to the busy shops so that we could choose our new clothes and shoes. This took about a week and then my mum and oldest sisters prepared the cakes for the celebration. About fifty cakes were placed on trays, ready for the oven, cakes of different shapes and colours: t'cherek (shaped like a crescent moon), bakalaua (like a diamond and golden in colour), tziriat (a little vase full of almonds), kinedlet and ryache (pink and dusted with icing sugar). Then me and my brother and my older sister had to carry the trays to le boulanger (the baker) so that he would put them in his big oven and bake them for us. We could carry a tray on our head, or under our arm. Sometimes I carried one under each arm and we strode into the street, ready to fight our way into the baker's shop.

The street was like a river floating with trays as everybody made their way to the baker's. We had to push our way into the queue and jostle each other to get into the shop. Inside, it was crammed with people and sweltering hot and there was a hubbub of talking. The baker would be standing there, red-faced, in his vest and with a hanky round his head. When you got to the head of the queue, he gave you a number and put the same number on your tray, ready for the oven. Sometimes he told you that you had to wait till someone came to collect their tray, because all the spaces were taken. The oven was huge and sometimes it was heated with a wood fire, which made the cakes taste wonderful. There was such a

Village Stories

rich aroma, it made you feel hungry. Two hours later, or even the next day, depending on how busy the baker was, we had to collect the trays.

While we were at the bakers, my mum cleaned the house and changed the curtains. On Eid eve, she bathed us one by one and then we all got into our pyjamas and went into the kitchen, not for dinner, but to get some henna on our hands. My mother put the dark powder into a copper tassa, with a pinch of sugar to make it sweet, and mixed it with water. Then with her four fingers she smoothed it on to our hands in whatever designs we wanted – circles, or over the whole hand, or two fingers for a man. One of my sisters liked to have her feet done too. As she applied the henna, my mum sang - about the henna, and about the prophet. Then we put on cotton mittens and went to bed. The henna was dark orange and green in colour and it would turn more orange or red. If it was very red, you had a good heart.

Then we went to sleep, waiting for the sun to rise so we could eat the lovely cakes and get dressed and go out near the house to show each other our new clothes and vote who was wearing the nicest ones. We played and had fun and a lot of guests arrived and they would give us money and I would save it to buy something nice.

Faisal

My neighbour Faisal had the mind of a child. He was not aggressive, but, when I was a child, because he looked a bit strange, I was afraid of him. We lived on the sixth floor and he lived on one of the floors below us, the third I think. When I came home from school at five o'clock, he would stay in the dark to frighten me. None of my school friends lived in the building, so I had to come up the stair myself. The lift had been broken for a long time. I was frightened to pass the third floor because of

Village Stories

Faisal. So I stayed on the second floor a long time, until someone else came up and I could go up with them.

One day I had to wait for more than an hour because I knew he was waiting for me or any child, so that he could scare them. They were big floors and he hid behind the lift waiting for you to come up. I was very late and my mother was looking out for me. The school was very near my home, so she wondered where I had got to. After one hour, my mother sent my oldest sister to look for me and she found me on the second floor sitting on my bag waiting for someone else to come up the stairs. I had wet myself because I was so frightened. I told her I was frightened of Faisal on the third floor, but she told me there was nobody there, it was just my imagination. Because it was winter time, I was cold.

Next day I didn't go to school just to avoid having to come home past Faisal. Sometimes in the morning he would say: 'I will be waiting for you.' In winter time, I was often absent from school because of him. Luckily, we eventually moved to another house.

Tea or Coffee

A coffee pot and a tea pot are on the table, talking to each other.

Coffee Hi! What are you doing here on this table with me? You always follow me wherever I go. Go away!

Tea I don't follow you at all. It's you who follow me. I find you everywhere I go: shops, houses, parties, schools, offices. Stop following me. Nobody wants you. You are a very bad taste.

Coffee It's you who are a very bad taste. You need a lot of sugar to make you drinkable.

Tea You get people very nervous and they can't sleep at night and children can't drink you at all

Coffee That's because I want to help them to work hard at night. And I'm more expensive than you. It's not everybody that can afford me. You are so much cheaper.

Tea That means I'm very popular. I'm for everybody. I'm so hospitable. You are selfish. You are only for one kind of people.

Village Stories

Coffee They import me from far away around the world: from Brazil, from Mexico, from Africa. All that costs a lot of money. I told you, it's not easy to get me.

Tea But you have a very bad smell.

Coffee It's not true. I've got a very nice smell. People can smell me from far away and I make them very pleased to drink me, especially in the morning. For example, Mrs Souidi can't get out in the morning before she drinks me. She is very addicted to me. If she doesn't drink me, she gets a very bad headache. I stop her headache and make her feel better. I get people ready for their work and give them a lot of energy.

Tea You mean that you make their blood pressure higher, then you make them sick. But me, I reduce cholesterol in their blood and I help fat people to lose weight.

Tea and *Coffee* argue for a long time. In the end they agree that each of them is liked by some people and each has a role in people's lives.

Mohamed is Rescued

Two years ago the handle of our toilet door was broken. I complained to GASS to try to get them to fix it, but they would not agree. They told me to do it myself. Not long after that, my son Mohamed, who was four years old, went into the toilet and closed the door. When he finished, he tried to open the door, but he couldn't. I was in the kitchen cooking lunch when suddenly I heard loud shouting and crying. I left everything and ran through to him. I found he was locked in the toilet and couldn't get the door open because of the broken handle. I tried to calm him and assure him that everything would be O.K. and I would rescue him, because he was in a panic.

I used a knife to try to open it, but it didn't work. Then I tried the handle of a spoon, but that didn't work either. Then I tried pushing on the door with my shoulder and then with my foot. I couldn't do it very well because I was nine months pregnant and I was worried in case I did any harm to my unborn baby.

After I had totally given up hope of rescuing my son by myself, I phoned 999 and told them that my son aged four years was locked in the toilet. After

Village Stories

only a few minutes, I heard the loud noise of a fire engine coming from far away. They pulled up right outside our door, and five firemen got out with equipment and ran up the path. I opened my door and found myself face to face with five very tall, strong firemen, all ready for their mission to save my son. One of them fired questions at me in a loud voice. 'Where is your son? What happened?' I was amazed by the way they looked. It was as if someone had told them my son was locked in the sky or somewhere like that.

I told them he was only locked inside the toilet. 'What!?' they said. 'Inside the toilet?' They all laughed and then one of them took a small key from his big bag and opened the door and found Mohamed with his trousers down and his eyes red from crying so much. 'Wash your hands,' the firemen told him. We were all laughing and very happy because Mohamed was safe.

I thanked them all and when they were going out the close, I noticed that a lot of people had gathered outside to watch the incident. I told them it was nothing serious and Mohamed was safe, and they all applauded the firemen.

After that incident, GASS agreed to repair the door handle, and they fitted a new one.

ZEYNEP GUNAY

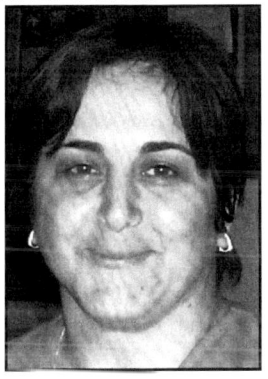

Kayser City

I grew up in Kayser City in Turkey. My father was an archaeologist who worked in a museum. He was the cleverest person in his family and he studied at university for many years. People who wanted to enter his profession or who wanted an answer to an archaeological problem would come and consult him. He died at his work, when the engine of a digger exploded on a site where he was working. I was only twelve at the time. Then, just before I was to get married, my mother died, so my eldest brother had to look after the family. He was a house-builder. I remember one of his stories

Village Stories

about the time he was working near a wooded area and he came upon a snake that fell in love with him! Or so he said. Anyway, it followed him everywhere, until one day another guy that was working on the house saw it and got such a fright that he jumped in the jeep and drove over it by accident.

School in Kayser City was very strict. If you didn't remember what you were supposed to do, the teacher had a stick and he would hit you with it. If you were in big trouble, you were sent to the head-teacher. He had a metal rod, and he heated it to frighten the children. But, if the teacher was in a good mood, I liked school. I left at seventeen and went to university and trained as a nurse. When I finished, I worked in a hospital, and that's what I did until I got out of Turkey and came to Britain.

It was always bad for Kurdish people in the town. The police often threatened us. My husband had a shop which sold alcohol. It often got attacked because of that, and because we were Kurdish and didn't go to the mosque. The police set fire to the shop. When my husband phoned the fire service, they didn't come; they said he had done it himself.

One night, the police came into our house and asked where my husband was. I told them he wasn't at home. They hit me with a rifle butt on my head and in the middle of my back, and knocked me down the stairs. I still feel the pain from that assault. It is hard to remember what happened then: I was so confused. They kept asking where my husband was and I just kept saying, 'I don't know.' When they found him, they beat him till he couldn't get up.

At night we managed to get away to Ankara. We hid there because we weren't safe in our house. Somebody could just have come and killed us. I was so shaken that I can't remember the details of getting there. Only that we went by lorry.

I was glad to come here to Scotland. At the present time, my health is not good. I have a sore head and I sleep most of the time because I am not working. When I learn things at college, I often forget them when I go home. But, when I eventually get my visa, I would like to be a nurse again. That's one thing I do remember – how to be a midwife and bring babies into the world.

Village Stories

JESRINA NASAR

Twenty Four Hours to Leave

The area of Sri Lanka where I lived had a lot of good things about it: good schools and hospitals and a good university at Jaffna. And Mannar, the island I was born in and grew up in, was a beautiful place. When we lived in Mannar, my father ran a coconut business. He had a lorry and a shop and people would phone up and place orders and he would go out and collect the coconuts and deliver them. Life was good till I was sixteen and the LTTE (Liberation Tigers of Tamil Eelam) made the proclamation that all Muslim people had to leave the island within twenty four hours.

So we had to get out and go to Chilaw. Before they drove us from the island, the LTTE searched through our possessions to see if we had any money. Fortunately, my father managed to hide a little. At first in Chilaw, we had to stay in a camp, which wasn't very good: it was very sandy, and it was difficult to cook and to eat. Eventually my father was able to find a house to rent and to follow his business again. There were a lot of coconuts in the Chilaw area, so he was able to expand and get a lorry and send orders to Colombo. My future husband was also there: he had come from Mannar at the same time as we had. So, for some time, things were alright in Chilaw. But after a while, the same threats appeared again, and once again there was no security for ordinary people. We had to get out.

Now that I am here in Glasgow, I miss having family around me. If I had my brothers and sisters, I would be very happy. When I had my baby last year, I was very tired. If some of my family had been with me for support, it would have made a big difference. My husband doesn't know how to do housework.

In Sri Lanka, there is no security and civilians are still dying. The LTTE problem won't go away, and on top of that there was the tsunami. One of my cousins lived near the beach and, when it struck, they

Village Stories

just had to run inland as far as they could. It was weeks before we heard that they were safe.

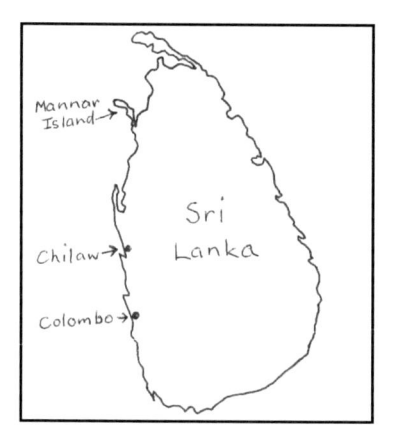

Map of Sri Lanka showing Mannar Island, Chilaw, and Colombo.

David Paul

His Grandfather's Hands
(extract from a novel)

Elijah and Sarah had an ordinary life on the surface, but inside the silence of each of them, a fire was always flaming; it burnt them, but they never spoke to each other about Andre after he was killed. They didn't open their hearts to each other at all.

That day Elijah had gone to look at the trees in the garden. He sat down beside the brook at the point where it branched into many little brooks which irrigated the trees. While he was playing with a little branch of olives, enjoying the sound of the dry leaves and the way they danced in the brook, his memory went back to a long time ago, when he was a child; he remembered once watching his grandfather sitting on the same spot playing with his finger in the water of the brook.

He remembered the way he squatted on the ground and how he asked him, 'do you see that dry leaf in the brook?'

Village Stories

'Yes,' he answered.

'After less than a minute you can't find it. Your grandfather's life has been like that. I don't know how it started. I don't know how I lost it.'

'I don't know what you mean, Grandpa.'

'Of course you don't know. But don't worry. After more experience, when you are older, you will understand what I have said.'

Eli remembered the hot weather of that day in summer, he remembered the sadness in his grandfather's voice.

He had said to six-year old Elijah, 'it is very hot, Sonny. I've always hated summers. But we're farmers, and farmers have always depended on water and hot summers. These are the heavenly gift to us.'

Then he put his hand on his knee and pushed himself up. Eli did the same. He had been sitting on the ground just like his grandfather and he pushed himself up in just the same way.

His grandfather took his hand and said, 'come on to the top of the garden, to the apple trees. I'm hungry. Aren't you hungry?'

'Yes, Grandpa. I am. Very much.'

They walked to the north part of the garden where the apple trees grew.

On the way, Eli copied his grandfather exactly, walking with the same tired strides, and he felt his big, calloused hand. All his attention was focussed on the old man's hands. At one point Eli stumbled and had to cling on to his grandfather. As the old man held on to him, he strained his arm, and so he had to take him by the other hand. But still Eli watched the thick vein on the back of his grandfather's hand. Then, quietly, he touched it.

'What are you doing, child?' his grandfather asked hesitantly.

'Nothing, Grandpa. I'm looking at your hand. Why is it rough? Why are the veins thick? Why are my hands not like yours?'

'Don't worry, dear,' said his grandfather. 'Days, Time and the World will give you these hands soon enough.'

'How soon, Grandpa? I like them,' he said with excitement.

'Don't be in a hurry. You will be given them very soon.'

Even six-year-old Eli was too heavy for his grandfather; he looked like a strong man, but inside he was broken. There was no strength in his hands.

He walked into the middle of the apple trees, look-

Village Stories

ing around for the best apples. Then he chose one, after touching it and examining it scrupulously. He took out the small knife he always carried in his pocket and very carefully he cut the apple.

'Why did you cut it so careful?' asked Eli.

'Because I don't want to hurt it. I know all of them, because I planted them and I've talked to them all my life.' Then he took Eli's hand and said, 'come, let's sit down together by the brook. It's a nice place. I like it there.'

Afterwards, when they were sitting at the same spot, where they had played with the bit of wood in the water, Eli watched silently while his grandfather peeled the apple.

'You are very lucky not to be the first born child,' his grandfather said.

'Why am I lucky, Grandpa?'

'Because you are not the first born.'

Eli was confused. 'Why am I lucky and he is not? I like my brother very much.'

'I know, but it does not concern your love.'

Eli was puzzled. 'Why am I then?' he asked again.

Grandpa gave him part of the peeled apple and said, 'I would tell you if you could understand it. But, I promise you, when you grow up, you will find out soon enough, because it will happen in your family too.'

After eating the apple they went home. On the way, Eli took his grandfather's hand and started to play with it.

In the Garden

It was about three o'clock in the afternoon on a hot day in the middle of summer. All my family were lying in the arbour. A large plate of cold water with a big piece of ice in the middle was at hand, and most of them were holding fans which from time to time they would waft in front of their faces. As is usual on summer afternoons in my city, it was quiet, because everybody was lying down. In that garden there were three generations and their children. (By 'children' I mean those who were under ten or twelve).

The adults were very comfortable because they had locked the garden door so that the children couldn't get out. But my granny wasn't thinking about the safety of the children. She was too worried about

Village Stories

me and my cousin Merriam. She was lying at a spot in the arbour where she could watch us easily.

At one point I heard Mum's voice. 'What are you doing, Grandma? Are you thirsty?'

'No,' she replied. 'Go for your nap.'

And everything was quiet except for the sound of a little breeze on the trees and the sweet fans on the faces of the adults, that made them all go into a deep nap, except, of course, for our poor granny.

Very quietly, I said to the children, 'I will give everyone of you a penny if you go to sleep. Anyone who doesn't sleep I will punish.'

My sweetest smallest cousin said, 'I don't feel like sleeping.'

'O.K.' I said, 'Just don't open your eyes and don't move.'

'O.K. If I don't move will you give me two pennies.'

I promised her. But while my sweet little cousin was speaking, Granny moved to behind the vine leaves from where she could get a good view of the rest of the garden.

'What's wrong, Grandma?' my mother said.

'Nothing. I just want to watch the shadows in the cherry tree.'

'Good. Just rest. I'm tired. In two hours I have to get up and make dinner for the family.

I knew that after Mum had spoken, Granny wouldn't say anything or do anything, because meal times were important for her. So Merriam and I walked a few steps away to a little hollow filled with dry leaves. We sat down and Merriam said, 'What do we do now?'

'I don't know. I suppose I take your hand.'

'It's better to kiss each other's mouth,' she said.

After a while, she said, 'isn't this better than just holding hands?'

'Of course,' I said, 'this is much better.'

Village Stories

Suddenly I felt my ear being twisted and I heard Granny's voice saying: 'it is better if you don't know about this big sin.'

'Don't tell his mum,' Merriam begged in a loud voice. 'She'll kill him.'

'Why should I kill my son?' said my mum.

After a few seconds Granny spoke. 'Because he didn't sleep.'

'You are all crazy!' said Mum. 'Everybody please go for a nap. Please!'

The Baby
(extract from a novel)

After about half an hour, the storm passed. Everything was quiet except for the sound of the baby crying. It didn't make sense, but it was crying and so it was alive.

The full moon came into view in the clear sky. By its light, Sarah could see that the woman was still there, with the wolf by her side, but quite far from the window. Still it was quiet except for the crying of the baby. Suddenly, the wolves were running after each other along the path past the window. For a second, one of them stopped and its eyes pierced through the window. Then it ran away after the others.

After a minute, Sarah could see neither the woman nor the wolves. Two lights were watching her, but she didn't see them. In that instant, she decided to go for the baby. She listened behind the door and heard quiet moaning. She thought to herself: it is unbelievable that a little baby could have survived among savage wolves. Her heart moved with compassion and pity. Suddenly the baby cried loudly. To Sarah it sounded like a beautiful voice singing a heavenly song. With tears in her eyes, she ran to the back room, shouting: 'I'm coming! Please survive!'

With her heart pounding, she snatched the rifle from the wall, and ran from the room back to the door. The groaning of the baby wasn't loud, but she could still hear it. With her finger on the rifle trigger, she unlocked the door and very gently edged it open. All she could see was a small bundle in a basket. She looked around but there was nothing else unusual; without any more hesitation, she dragged the basket inside and locked the door.

The first thing Sarah did was to pull the blanket aside to see the baby's face. As she did this, the baby

Village Stories

started to cry and move its hands. She laid the gun aside and took the baby over to the fire. To Sarah the wet blanket felt like soft silk and her heart grew tender; the crying of the baby was like heavenly music. Its face was wet, whether from rain or her tears she didn't know. She said something, she didn't know what, but she spoke with happiness and a smile on her face.